# IN MARY'S GARDEN

by Tina & Carson Kügler

Houghton Mifflin Harcourt

Boston  New York

## To Our Families

www.hmhco.com

The text of this book is set in Mr Eaves Sans.

Carson and Tina combine traditional watercolor with digital painting, collage, and vintage papers. While every effort was made to stay true to Mary's distinctive artistic style and vision, some liberties were taken with placement and chronology of her sculptures, and some designs were based on a combination of recurring motifs in Mary's work.

Mary's secret code on page 3 is inspired by the 1913 Naval Phonetic Alphabet.

Library of Congress Cataloging-in-Publication Data
Kügler, Tina, author, illustrator.
In Mary's garden / by Tina & Carson Kügler.
pages cm
ISBN 978-0-544-27220-0
1. Nohl, Mary, 1914–2001—Juvenile literature. 2. Nohl, Mary, 1914–2001—Homes and haunts—Wisconsin—Fox Point—Juvenile literature. 3. Environment (Art)—Wisconsin—Fox Point—Juvenile literature. 4. Outsider art—Wisconsin—Fox Point—Juvenile literature. I. Kügler, Carson, author, illustrator. II. Title.
N6537.N648K84 2015
709.2—dc23
2014009669

Manufactured in China
SCP 10 9 8 7 6 5 4 3 2 1
4500512290

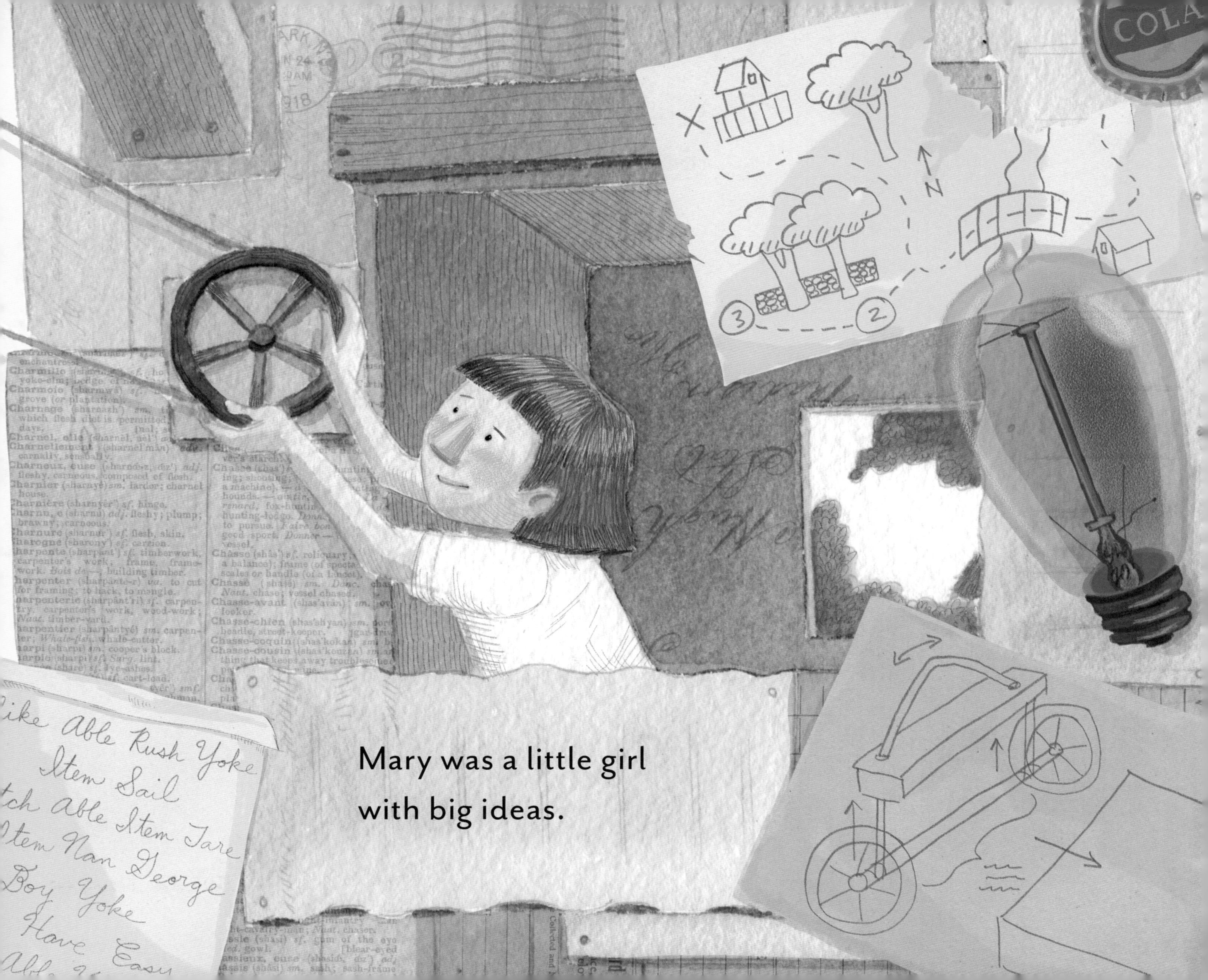


Mary was a little girl
with big ideas.

While the other girls
took cooking classes,

Mary tried woodworking.

She helped her father build a house
on the shore of Lake Michigan.

Mary was happiest when her hands were
busy making, building, creating things.

As she grew older, she
traveled all over the world
and drew everything she saw.

CARTE POST

CORRESPONDANCE

ADRE

Having a fine
trip! plenty of
adventures to
about
back

Basil & Sassafras

ch Dr.

WI

217

Mary fell in love with art.

AHU TONGARIKI, EASTER ISLAND

16 FOOT MOAI HEAD

But the Wisconsin winters
were long and cold . . .

. . . and she would often think of the bright colors
and wonderful things she had seen on her travels.

One spring morning,
Sassafras and Basil discovered
a marvelous creature
washed up on the sand.

Only, it was just a little piece of him.

But Mary understood.

Together, they found more.

Then they loaded up their bumpy
red wagon and headed home.

Over the next few days, they
found another scrap here,

another jumbled
lump there.

Mary loved to
collect things
she found.

And she knew
just how to
use them.

Mary mixed cement with beach sand, like her father had shown her many years before.

She spread the cement over a support she built of wood, pipes, and chicken wire.

The dogs watched curiously
as the creature grew.

Mary dragged an old comb over the wet cement to make textures.

She carefully covered the creature with beach glass, smooth stones, shells, and driftwood.

It took a long time to put together all the odds and ends and bits and bobs, but finally Mary was done.

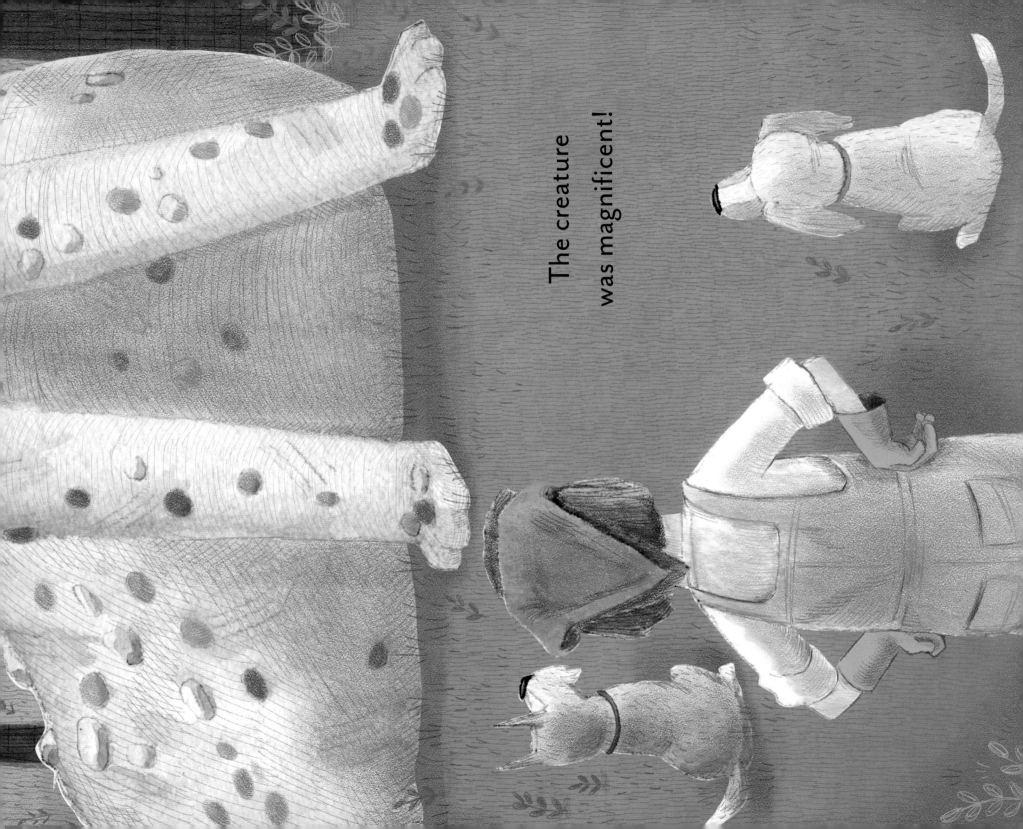

The creature was magnificent!

But Sassafras thought he looked a little lonely.

Mary agreed.

Basil brought the wagon.

And the three of them went
back to the beach and found
another wonderful creature

waiting for them on the sand.

Only, it was just a
little piece of her.

And one piece led to another . . .

. . . until creature after creature

leapt and crawled and danced

from Mary's imagination

and into . . .

. . . her garden.

Mary always had room for one more stone, one more shell, and one more friend.

The Wisconsin artist Mary Nohl (1914–2001) spent her summers with her family at their Lake Michigan cottage.

In 1928, when she was thirteen, her model airplane won first prize in her industrial arts class. She was one of only two girls in the class.

At age twenty-four, Mary graduated from the School of the Art Institute of Chicago. She became an art teacher, and later ran a small pottery studio. Mary also traveled to Mexico, Guatemala, Europe, and Africa. (She crossed the ocean twelve times in twelve years!) She took her sketchbook everywhere and drew everything she saw.

In 1943, her family's beloved lakeside cottage was remodeled for year-round use, and Mary moved back to live by the lake with her parents.

In the 1960s, her elderly mother and father passed away. Out of her loss came hope: because her parents left her the cottage she loved and an inheritance to live comfortably, Mary became financially independent. She could now dedicate all of her time to making art.

Mary loved dogs, and had them as constant companions throughout her life. Sassafras and Basil were her dogs during the time period of this book.

During the cold Wisconsin winters, Mary's art transformed

the inside of her house. She covered the walls with paintings. She melted down the family's silverware to make jewelry. She painted every surface, including the furniture and carpeting, with bold swirls and spatters. "So I won't have to vacuum so often," she would say. "The cracker crumbs won't show." When the weather was warm, huge sculptures rose from her yard.

Visitors came from all over to marvel at Mary's wonderful garden and home. No one had ever seen anything like it.

Some people didn't understand Mary's unusual creations, and called her a witch. A few even threw stones at her windows, but Mary wasn't deterred. After vandals destroyed two of her sculptures, she used the pieces to make more art: the remaining support posts became the front legs of a smiling twelve-foot dinosaur!

Making art made Mary truly happy. She wasn't interested in selling her art or being famous. She made art for herself.

Even today, Mary's art is controversial. Her affluent neighbors consider the traffic generated by onlookers to be a nuisance, demanding Mary's beloved home and creations be dismantled and relocated. The John Michael Kohler Art Center in Sheboygan, Wisconsin, is seeking to preserve her legacy, and we hope Mary's extraordinary art will be enjoyed and cherished for generations to come.

Sources:

"Artist's Whimsies Overflow Home." *Milwaukee Journal*, September 29, 1968.

Manger, Barbara, and Janine Smith. *Mary Nohl Inside and Outside.* Milwaukee: Greater Milwaukee Foundation/University of Wisconsin Press, 2008.

"Mary Nohl: Artist and Yard-ist." *Lakeshore Guide*, 2–4. September 1984.

"Nights of Vandalism Haunt Fox Point Home." *Milwaukee Journal*, March 6, 1979.

Umberger, Leslie. *Mary Nohl: A Life in Art.* Sheboygan, Wis.: John Michael Kohler Arts Center exhibition catalog, 2002.

Photo credits:

Photo on lower left by *Milwaukee Journal-Sentinel*, photo on upper right by Tina Kügler.